Native American Recipes

By Mary Ruth Hughes
Illustrations by Gina Cruz-Rider

Text copyright © 2013 Mary Ruth Hughes
Illustration copyright © 2013 Gina Cruz-Rider

Library of Congress Cataloging-in-Publication Data

All rights reserved. No part of this book may be reproduced in any manner without the express written consent of the author and illustrator, except in the case of brief excerpts in critical reviews and articles.

Willow Vista Books
www.WillowVistaBooks.com

Warning: Recipes in this book have been collected from very old, old and modified recipes. Some recipes in this book call for raw eggs, nuts, peanut oil and other ingredients that can be lethal to persons with food allergies or weakened immune systems. The author and illustrator of this book shall be held harmless and are not responsible for any loss or damage incurred, or alleged to have incurred, directly or indirectly, by using these ingredients. Use substitution ingredients if this is a concern.

Printed in the United States of America

FIRST EDITION
2013

ISBN-10: 1482017016   ISBN-13: 978-1482017014

NATIVE AMERICAN RECIPES

Table of Contents

1. Apache
2. Aztec
3. Caddo
4. Cherokee
5. Cheyenne
6. Chickasaw
7. Choctaw
8. Comanche
9. Cree
10. Delaware
11. Hopi
12. Kickapoo
13. Kiowa
14. Mandan
15. Muscogee Creek
16. Natchez
17. Navajo
18. Nez Perce
19. Osage
20. Pima
21. Pueblo
22. Quapaw
23. Sac and Fox
24. Seminole
25. Shawnee
26. Shoshone
27. Sioux
28. Wichita
29. Yaqui
30. Zuni

APACHE

(Ndee)
Meaning: The people

Apaches are native to the southwest deserts of the United States. This area now encompasses the states of Arizona, New Mexico and Texas. Some Apache people were also located across the border into northern Mexico. There is no single tribal headquarters for all parts of the Apache Indian Nation in the United States. There are several different groups of Apache people. Three tribes are listed below. Each one has their own tribal offices and headquarters located in Arizona.

* Yavapai   *White Mountain   *San Carlos

Acorn Stew

Cut 2 ½ to 3 pounds of round steak into bite-size pieces. Place a small amount of cooking oil in the bottom of a stew pan and heat until it is sizzling hot. Add meat and cook until brown on all sides. Add water to cover meat and simmer over a low flame for about three hours until meat is tender. Salt to taste. Shell sweet acorns and grind them into very fine flour until you have about ¾ cup. Strain the broth from the meat and set aside. Shred meat and place in a large glass bowl along with ¾ cup of acorn flour. Pour the hot broth (you set aside) over the meat and acorn flour mixture and stir. Stew is ready to serve in individual bowls. Fry bread is sometimes served with the stew.

Acorn flour can be purchased on the internet. When you search acorn flour, several sites for purchasing are listed.

AZTEC

(Aeztek)
Meaning: Person from Aztian

The Aztec people are indigenous to central Mexico. It is generally thought that in ancient times Aztlan was somewhere north of the Valley of Mexico. Some experts have placed it as far north as the southwest Untied States. The Aztec headquarters today are located in Mexico City, Mexico.

Taco Meat

2 pounds chuck roast cut into large chunks
2 pounds country style pork rib chunks without bones
1 small can diced green chili peppers
1 can of diced tomatoes (16 oz.)
1 diced onion
2 tablespoons salt
¼ cup taco seasoning
1 tablespoon black pepper

Put all ingredients into a large pot and add enough water to cover meat. Put lid on pot and cook over a low flame 2-3 hours or until meat is tender and juice has been partially absorbed. Drain meat and shred using two forks to pull meat apart. Meat should be tender enough to shred easily.

Tacos

1 package corn tortillas
skillet half full of cooking oil (I use peanut oil)

Warm tortillas so they don't crack when folded. Place meat in center of tortilla and fold in half. Fry in hot oil until crispy. Fill with diced onions, lettuce and cheese. Top with a ripe olive and sour cream. Add salsa to taste. Recipe for salsa is on the Navajo page.

CADDO

(Kadohadacho)
Meaning: True Chiefs

The Caddo people are indigenous to Texas, Oklahoma, Arkansas and Louisiana. They are a federally recognized tribe. In the past, the Caddo people living in Texas mined salt from underground mines which they boiled down to use in their cooking. The Caddo people were hunters and farmers. Their food consisted of cornbread, soups and stews. Caddo men hunted deer, buffalo and small game. They caught fish from the rivers. Today, the Caddo Nation headquarters are located in Binger, Oklahoma.

Wild Onions and Scrambled Eggs

| bundle of wild onions | 2 tablespoons bacon grease |
| 8-12 eggs | salt to taste |

Cut onions into segments. Heat bacon grease in skillet and add onions. Cook until onions are transparent. Add enough water to halfway cover the onions. Simmer with the lid on skillet until tender. Drain off water and stir in the eggs. Mix eggs and onions thoroughly and cook until done. Add salt to taste. Serve hot.

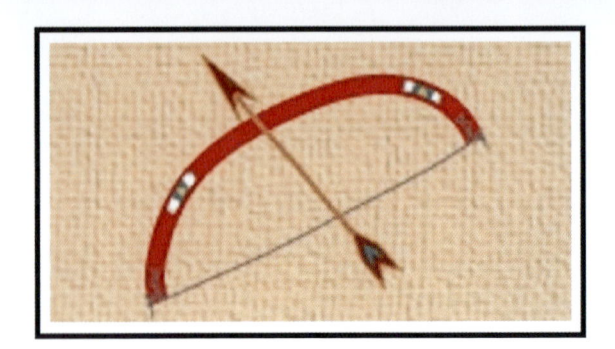

CHEROKEE

(Tsalagi)
Meaning: Principal People

The Cherokee people are indigenous to the Southeastern United States. They lived in Georgia, Alabama, Tennessee and the Carolinas before being removed to Indian Territory in the 1830's. Their long trek to Indian Territory is known as the "Trail of Tears". The Cherokee language has an innovative writing system that was invented by the Cherokee scholar Sequoyah. Cherokee tribal headquarters are located in Tahlequah, Oklahoma.

Cherokee Catfish

catfish filets * yellow cornmeal * salt * peanut oil

Place catfish filets on cutting board and blot with a paper towel to get off excess moisture. Salt each piece of fish on both sides. Sprinkle cornmeal over filets and coat thoroughly. Pour enough peanut oil in the bottom of a cast iron skillet so that the fish will float while cooking. Heat oil until it is hot and sizzles when a pinch of corn meal is thrown in the oil. Fry the fish until it is golden brown on both sides and then place on a wire rack to drain off the oil or blot with paper towels. Eat while hot.

Hush puppies

1 ½ cups self-rising cornmeal
½ cup self-rising flour
½ teaspoon salt
1 small onion, grated

1 cup buttermilk
1 egg slightly beaten
peanut oil

In a medium size bowl mix cornmeal, flour, baking soda and salt. Stir in onion. In a small bowl mix the buttermilk and egg. Pour buttermilk mixture into the dry ingredients and stir until blended. Heat 2" peanut oil in skillet to 350 degrees F. Drop a tablespoon full of batter in hot oil and fry until golden brown. Cook in small batches. Drain on paper towels. Serve hot!

CHEYENNE

(Tsitsistas)
Meaning: The people of alien speech

The Cheyenne people roamed the Great Plains of America in what are now the states of South Dakota, Wyoming, Nebraska, Colorado and Kansas. The Cheyenne people were good horsemen. The United States government forced the Cheyennes to move to Oklahoma during the 1800's. Some escaped this forced migration and fled to Montana. Montana Cheyenne headquarters are located in Lame Deer, Montana. Oklahoma Cheyenne headquarters are located in Concho, Oklahoma.

Buffalo Steaks

2 large buffalo steaks, any cut
2 large wild onions
Salt
lard or cooking oil

Place buffalo steaks on a flat clean rock or cutting board. Pound steaks with another stone until all the fibers have been broken down to tenderize meat. Sprinkle a little salt over the steaks. Cut wild onions in half. On the cut side, rub the onions and salt into the meat. Repeat on other side of meat. Drop lard or oil on stone or skillet and let it float out until you have a well-greased spot large enough to place the steaks on. Cook for 14-20 minutes on each side. If you have extra wild onions, slice thin strips and fry with steaks.

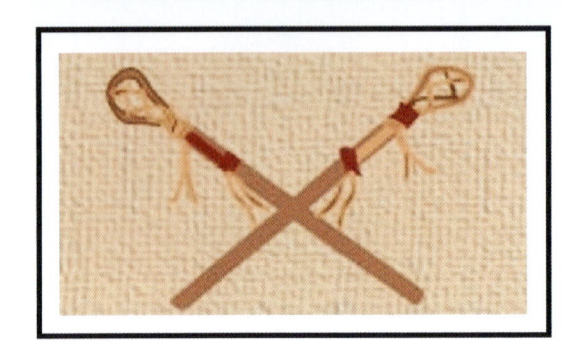

CHICKASAW

(Chi-kash-sha)
Meaning: Name of a legendary Chickasaw leader

The Chickasaw people are indigenous to the southeastern woodlands of the United States. They were removed from their homelands in Mississippi to Indian Territory in 1838. They came to a place they called "Good Springs". They built a town around the springs and called it Tishomingo after their last Great War chief. Tishomingo became the capitol of the Chickasaw Nation. Today the Chickasaw headquarters are located in Ada, Oklahoma.

Pashofa

Pashofa is a stew made with white pearl corn or hominy and fresh pork. In ancient times a pashofa ceremony was held to heal the sick. Today, pashofa is served at ceremonial and social events.

Traditional Recipe

- large cast iron kettle
- one gallon of white cracked pashofa corn
- three gallons of water
- five pounds of fresh pork

Rinse corn and soak in cold water for two hours. Rinse again and soak for another two hours. Rinse one last time and add three gallons of water. Bring the corn to a boil. Reduce heat to a low simmer. Add fresh pork roast cut into pieces. Simmer the corn and pork for at least eight hours stirring now and then to keep the corn from sticking to the bottom of the pot. Add salt to taste when done.

Modern Recipe

Brown chunks of fresh pork in lard at the bottom of the pot. Pork chops or bacon can be for added flavor. Cook pork until thoroughly done. Add drained hominy and enough water to make soupy. Bring to a boil and simmer for a half hour. Salt to taste.

CHOCTAW

(Chah-tah)
Meaning: Name of a legendary Choctaw leader

The Choctaw people are indigenous to the southeastern woodlands of the United States. Legends say that Chickasaws and Choctaws are related. They are believed to have descended from two brothers: Chah-tah and Chi-kash-sha. The Choctaws were removed from their homelands in Alabama and Mississippi to Indian Territory in the 1830's. Today, the Choctaw Nation headquarters are located in Durant, Oklahoma.

Choctaw Hunters Stew

2 pounds deer meat
(you can substitute beef roast or hamburger meat)
1 medium size chopped onion
4 stalks chopped celery
1 can whole kernel corn
(or fresh corn cut off the cob)
2 cans of diced tomatoes with juice

3 sliced carrots
4 medium diced potatoes
3 cups cabbage
1 cup sliced mushrooms
2 chopped garlic cloves
2 tablespoons beef
   bouillon granules
3-4 cups water

Brown meat in bottom of cooking pot using a little oil or lard. Not necessary to use oil if using hamburger meat. When meat is slightly brown, add onion and celery. Continue browning meat with onions and celery. When onions are transparent, add the following ingredients to the meat mixture. One can corn, tomatoes with juice, carrots, potatoes, cabbage, mushrooms, garlic, beef bouillon and water. You won't need salt if you use bouillon. Use black pepper to taste. Cook until potatoes and carrots are soft. Stew is now ready to eat. Refrigerate leftovers. This stew is better the second day.

COMANCHE

(Numinu)
Meaning: The people

The Comanche are indigenous to the southern plains of the United States. Their historic territory consisted of present day eastern New Mexico, southern Colorado, northeastern Arizona, southern Kansas, all of Oklahoma and most of northwest Texas. Historically, the Comanche were hunter-gatherers with a horse culture.
Their headquarters are located at: 584 North West Bingo Road, Lawton, Oklahoma.

Comanche Fried Frog Legs

2 pounds frog legs
½ cup lard or cooking oil
1 well-beaten egg
½ teaspoon salt
½ cup cornmeal
¼ teaspoon pepper
Small amount of water

Mix cornmeal, egg, salt and pepper together with enough water to form a batter. Heat oil in an iron skillet. Dip frog legs into the batter to coat all sides. Drop frog legs into hot oil and cook until they are brown on all sides.

CREE

(Lyiniwok or Ininiwok)
Meaning: The people

Cree people are indigenous to Canada and parts of the northern United States. North Dakota and Montana were considered Cree territory. Cree people from prairie regions are known as the Plains Cree. Those who live in the forested land are known as the Woodland Cree. Native Indian bands are called First Nations in Canada and Tribes in the United States. Chippewa Cree Tribal headquarters are located at Box Elder, Montana

Pemmican
(A Cree word for rendered fat.)

Pemmican is a dried mixture of meat, berries and rendered fat (suet or tallow). Pemmican can last for several months to several years without refrigeration. A perfect survival food.

4 cups lean meat (deer, beef, caribou or moose)
3 cups dried fruit
2 cups rendered fat
unsalted nuts
honey: as much as needed to bind ingredients together

Double grind lean meat. Spread meat thin on a cookie sheet and dry at 180 degrees F. This process takes at least 8 hours to be crispy. Pound meat into a powder using a blender or food processor. Set meat aside in a large bowl. Grind dried fruit leaving a few chunks for texture and place in bowl with meat. Heat rendered fat on stove at medium heat until it turns to liquid. Don't burn!

Add liquid fat to meat and fruit then add nuts and honey. Mix ingredients by hand until thoroughly mixed. Let cool and store.

DELAWARE

(Lenape)
Meaning: The people

The Delaware people were indigenous to the mid-Atlantic area of the United States known today as New Jersey, Delaware, New York and Pennsylvania. In the late 1800's, the Delaware Tribe was relocated to Indian Territory which later became Oklahoma. Their tribal headquarters are located in Bartlesville, Oklahoma.

Delaware Deer Liver with Onions

1 venison liver, sliced
(substitute calf's liver if you prefer)
3 cups boiling water
4 tablespoons flour
½ teaspoon salt
¼ teaspoon pepper
4 tablespoons bacon fat
2 cups wild onions, sliced
1 can mushroom soup
1 can of water

Trim and wash the liver and slice into ¼ inch slices. Pour half of the boiling water over the slices, drain and repeat with the rest of the boiling water.
Drain and pat dry. On bread board, mix the flour, salt and pepper. Roll the liver slices in the flour mixture until thoroughly covered. Over high heat, heat the bacon fat in a skillet until blue smoke appears. Add liver and sauté on both sides until lightly browned. Remove the liver and set aside. Add the thinly sliced onions to skillet and cook over medium heat until golden brown. Add one can mushroom soup then fill the can with warm water and add it to the skillet. Add liver to the mixture in the skillet, cover and cook on low for 1 ½ hours. Make sure the pan does not cook dry. Serve with mashed potatoes and melted bacon grease as gravy.

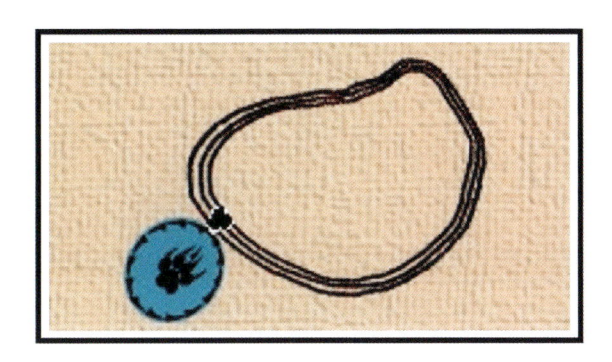

HOPI

(Ho'pitu)
Meaning: Peaceful Person

The Hopi people are indigenous to the highlands of northern Arizona. They have continued to inhabit the same place for millennium. Today their headquarters are located in Kykotsmovi, Arizona.

Hopi Scalloped Red Peppers

4 cups white corn kernels
2 red peppers finely chopped
1 can cream of celery soup
(What did they use before canned soup was invented?)
½ cup evaporated milk
1 teaspoon salt
½ teaspoon dry mustard
1 ½ cup seasoned bread (stuffing)
½ cup melted butter

Put corn and red peppers in a small cooking pot. Add soup, milk, salt and mustard. Stir over low heat. Melt butter and mix into the bread stuffing. Line the bottom of a 9" x 6" baking dish with half the mixture. Pour corn mixture over the stuffing and cover with remaining stuffing. Bake in a 375 F. degree oven for about 30 minutes. Serve with pork chops or fried ham.

KICKAPOO

(Kikapoo, Kikapu)
Meaning: Wanderer

"Kickapoo" is thought to be a corruption of a Shawnee word for "wanderers". The Kickapoos are indigenous to Michigan, Wisconsin and Illinois. Most Kickapoos left their native lands and moved southward to Kansas, Oklahoma, Texas and Mexico. Headquarters for the Kansas Kickapoo tribe are located in Horton, Kansas.

Pugna
(Baked cornbread)

1 cup yellow cornmeal	½ cup milk
½ cup flour	1 egg
1 teaspoon salt	½ teaspoon baking soda
1 tablespoon baking powder	¼ cup butter or shortening
1 cup buttermilk	2 tablespoons butter or shortening

Preheat oven to 450 degrees. Combine cornmeal, flour, salt and baking powder in a large bowl. Mix. In a small bowl add buttermilk and milk. Add egg and stir with a fork. Add baking soda and stir. Melt ¼ cup of butter or shortening and slowly add to batter. Stir only enough to combine ingredients. In a cast iron skillet, melt 2 tablespoons of butter or shortening. Pour the batter into the hot skillet. Spread to even the batter. Cook on stovetop for one minute. Bake 20-25 minutes until brown. Edges will be crispy.

KIOWA

(Gaigwu)
Meaning: Kiowa people

The Kiowa people are indigenous to the Great Plains of the United States. Originally they lived in the area that is now known as Montana. They migrated to the Southern Plains in the early 1800's. In 1867 the Kiowa were moved to a reservation in southwestern Indian Territory now known as Oklahoma. Headquarters for the Kiowa people are located in Carnegie, Oklahoma.

Venison Roast

slab of venison (or beef) about 2" thick
1 chopped medium size onion
4 teaspoons bacon fat
¼ teaspoon pepper
½ teaspoon salt or garlic salt
½ cup flour
2-3 cups water

Lay venison on cutting board and sprinkle salt and pepper on both sides. Coat each side with flour. Melt fat in a large frying pan and brown roast. Cook onions with meat until slightly brown. Pour water over roast. Cover and let simmer until meat is tender and can be pulled apart with a fork.

MANDAN

(Mi ah'ta nes)
(People on the river bank)

Mandan people were indigenous to the area around the Missouri River and its tributaries in present day North and South Dakota. The Mandans were more settled than the other nomadic tribes of the Great Plains. Bison was their main food. It was supplemented by agriculture and trade. The Mandan people were plagued with small pox. It was brought to them by the European fur traders. Mandans had no resistance to the disease and very few survived. Mandan tribal headquarters are located in New Town, North Dakota.

Sunflower Seed Soup

2 cups shelled sunflower seeds   1 teaspoon salt
3 sliced green onions   6 cups chicken broth

Simmer all ingredients for one hour. Serve hot.

MUSCOGEE CREEK

(Este Mvskokvlke)
Meaning: Swamp or wet ground

The Muscogee Creek people are indigenous to the southeastern woodlands of the United States. They were removed from their homelands to Indian Territory in the late 1830's. Today, the Creek Nation headquarters are located in Okmulgee, Oklahoma

Wild Grape/ Blue Dumplings

3 pints wild possum grapes
2 cups flour
3 ½ teaspoons baking powder
1 teaspoon shortening or lard
3 tablespoons sugar
1 egg
½ teaspoon salt
milk

Possum grapes grow wild along the creek banks in the southern United States. Today, possum grapes are scarce so you can substitute Concord grape juice. Rendering the juice from possum grapes was done by cooking grapes in just enough water to cover them. They were cooked until the water boiled. Then the grapes were mashed and strained through a clean cloth or sieve. Possum grapes are very tart. Sugar can be added if needed. Store bought Concord grape juice is usually sweet so it isn't necessary to add more sugar. Pour juice into a large sauce pan and set aside.

In a large mixing bowl add flour, sugar, baking powder and salt. Mix shortening into dry mixture with your fingers. When thoroughly mixed, add egg and enough milk to make a stiff dough.

Bring juice to a boil and drop dough into the boiling juice one spoonful at a time. Cover with a lid and cook for about 15-20 minutes or until dough is done in the middle. Serve dumplings hot in individual bowls with an ample amount of juice.

NATCHEZ

(Notch-ay)
Meaning: Red crawfish people

The Natchez people are indigenous to the southeastern woodlands of the United States along the Mississippi River valley. The area today is located in the states of Mississippi and Louisiana. The Natchez were mound builders. Today, many Natchez mounds can be found near Natchez, Mississippi. The Natchez tribe was defeated by the French in the early 1700's, and the survivors scattered. Descendants of the Natchez people live in many different places today, but most of them live among the Chickasaw, Creek and Cherokee tribes of Oklahoma. Natchez tribal headquarters are located at 70 Bluff Road, Olympia Village Columbia, South Carolina.

Natchez PawPaw Pie

(*The* pawpaw *is a tropical-type fruit native to the temperate woodlands of the southeastern United States.*)

1 cup sugar
1 cup milk
1 egg
¼ teaspoon salt
1 tablespoon flour
1-1/2 cups pawpaws, peeled and seeded

Place all ingredients into stew pan and stir together. Cook over medium heat until thickened. Pour into unbaked pie shell and bake until crust is done. Can be topped with meringue or whipped cream.

(If pawpaws are unavailable, you can substitute mangos or bananas.)

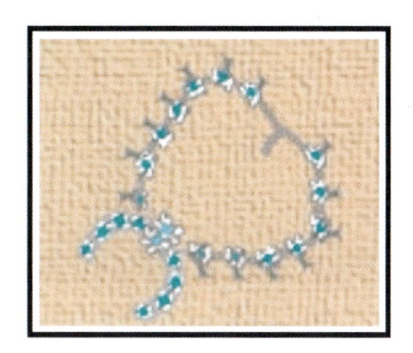

NAVAJO

(Diné)
Meaning: The people

The Navajo people are indigenous to the states of Utah, Arizona and New Mexico. Their reputation for making beautiful silver and turquoise jewelry is known throughout the world. The Navajo Nation headquarters and government offices are in close proximity to the mystical Window Rock formation in Arizona.

Fry Bread

3 cups flour 2 teaspoons salt
2 ½ tablespoons baking powder warm water
shortening or lard the size of a large walnut skillet half full of shortening or lard

Mix dry ingredients in a large bowl. With fingers, mix and work shortening into dry mixture until it disappears. Add enough warm water to make a soft dough ball. Let sit 20 minutes. Pinch off a piece of dough the size of a large lemon and roll it on a floured bread board with a rolling pin. The thickness of the dough should be about a quarter of an inch thick. Heat cooking oil. Drop dough into hot oil and cook until golden brown on both sides. The dough will puff up as it cooks. Serve HOT with honey, powdered sugar, cinnamon sugar or use as a base for Indian tacos.

Salsa

Pour two cans of mini-diced tomatoes with juice into a medium size mixing bowl. Add 1 medium size diced red onion, ½ bunch of chopped cilantro, 1 bunch of chopped green onions using small amount of the green stalks, 3 medium size fresh diced tomatoes and two diced jalapeno peppers. Add ½ teaspoon garlic salt, 1 teaspoon garlic granules and 4 finely chopped garlic cloves. Mix ingredients and crush with a potato masher. Refrigerate.

Indian Tacos

On individual pieces of cooked frybread, spread refried beans over the entire surface. Sprinkle prepared meat (beef, pork, hamburger) on top of the beans. Add chopped onions, tomatoes and lettuce. Top with salsa and shredded cheese.

NEZ PERCE

(Nimiipuu)
Meaning: Pierced nose

The Nez Perce people were indigenous to the Pacific Northwest which now encompasses the states of Idaho, Oregon and Washington. Nez Perce are excellent horsemen and are noted for breeding the Appaloosa horse. Nez Perce tribal headquarters are located in Lapwai, Idaho.

Wild Pacific Salmon

Thoroughly season salmon filets on each side with garlic salt, cayenne pepper and black pepper. Oil skillet (lightly) with cooking oil. Heat pan over medium/hot flame. When water droplets sizzle in the pan, it is ready to seer salmon. Add filets and turn burner down to low/medium heat. Drizzle maple syrup over filets, cover pan and cook for four minutes. Flip filets, apply syrup to flipped side. Cover and cook for another 4 minutes or until done. Serve with fresh vegetables.

Salmon can baked on a cedar plank of wood if preferred.

OSAGE

(Wah-zah-zhoy)
Meaning: Little ones of the middle waters

Osage people are indigenous to the Ohio River Valley in present day Kentucky. They migrated west of the Mississippi River to Arkansas, Missouri, Kansas and Oklahoma in the 1600's. The Osage are a federally recognized tribe. Their tribal headquarters are located in Pawhuska, Oklahoma.

Osage Sweet Corn Pudding

12 ears fresh corn
1 tablespoon sugar
1 quart milk
2 tablespoons flour

1 tablespoon butter
3 eggs
salt to taste

Grate and scrape corn in a large bowl or pan. (I use a sharp knife to cut the tips off the kernels and then I scrape the cob with the knife to get all the inside out of the kernel.) Add milk. Set aside. In a small bowl, cream flour and butter. Add sugar and well-beaten egg yolks. Stir these ingredients into the corn and milk mixture. Add salt to taste. In a separate bowl beat egg whites until stiff peaks form. Gently fold egg whites into mixture and bake in a well-buttered cake pan. Bake at 350 degrees F. until golden brown.

PIMA

O'Odham) (Tohono O'Odham)
Meaning: River people   *Meaning: Desert people*

The Pima tribe descended from the Hohokam people, meaning: "those who have gone". The Hohokam were a prehistoric group of people who originated in Mexico. Migrating from Mexico, the Pima settled north of Mexico in what is now Arizona. Their land is where the Gila River and the Salt River meet in Arizona. Pima women are noted for their watertight woven baskets. Headquarters for two Pima tribes are:

Ak Chin Indian Community Council   Gila River Indian Community Council
   42507 W. Peters and Nail Road   P.O. Box 97
      Maricopa, AZ 85239   Sacaton, AZ 85247

Cheese Enchiladas

¼ cup vegetable oil
5 tablespoons flour
4 cups chicken broth or water
2 tablespoons chili powder

1 dozen large corn tortillas
1 medium size block of cheddar cheese
salt to taste
1 finely chopped medium size onion

13" X 9" rectangular glass baking dish

Grate cheese and dice onion. Set aside. Over medium flame, heat oil in a large skillet. Add flour and stir with a whisk until flour is slightly brown. Pour broth into flour mixture and continue stirring with the whisk. Add chili powder and salt. Turn heat to simmer. Cook sauce until it is the consistency of thin gravy, stirring constantly. Set aside. Place tortillas on a plate and microwave for 20 seconds. Tortillas should be warm not mushy. Take one tortilla at a time, dip into sauce and place on a plate. Fill each tortilla with grated cheese and a small amount of onion. Roll tortilla keeping cheese and onion in the middle. Place one at a time in baking dish. Cover tortillas with remaining sauce. Sprinkle remaining cheese and onion over the top. Bake in oven or microwave until cheese is melted. Serve hot!

PUEBLO

(Pueb-lo)
Meaning: Village

The Pueblo people are indigenous to the southwestern United States. Their traditional economy was based on agriculture and trade in the 18th century. When encountered by Europeans, they were living in villages that the Spanish called pueblos, meaning "towns". The best known pueblo people are Taos, Acoma, Zuni and Hopi. These tribes are located in New Mexico and Arizona.

Calabacitas

3 ears fresh corn
1 slice of bacon cut into small pieces
1 tablespoon butter
1 teaspoon minced garlic
2 cups cubed yellow summer squash
2 cups cubed green zucchini squash
½ cup thinly sliced green onions
½ cup roasted chopped green chili peppers
salt to taste
½ cup diced fresh tomatoes
1/3 cup coarsely chopped fresh cilantro
1 cup chopped medium size onion

Cook bacon in a large skillet over medium-high flame. Reduce fire and add butter. Sauté onion for about 2 minutes. Add garlic and continue cooking for 2 more minutes stirring frequently. Add yellow and green squash and cook for 4 minutes. Stir frequently. Add chopped onions and chili pepper. Cook slightly. Don't overcook tomatoes. Garnish with chopped green onions and cilantro.

QUAPAW

(Uga'khpa)
Meaning: Downstream people

The Quapaw people were mainly indigenous to the west side of the Mississippi River in what is now Arkansas. They were also known to have inhabited the western parts of Missouri, Mississippi and Tennessee throughout history. The Quapaw people were removed from their homelands in the 1800's along with many other tribes to Indian Territory. Indian Territory became the state of Oklahoma in 1907. Today, Quapaw headquarters are located in Quapaw, Oklahoma.

Quapaw Fried Rabbit

1 rabbit, skinned and washed   1 cup flour
1 teaspoon salt   pepper to taste
cooking oil   1 diced onion
juice from ½ lemon

Cut rabbit into pieces. Salt and pepper each piece then roll in flour until thoroughly covered. Cover bottom of skillet with cooking oil and heat until it sizzles when a pinch of flour is added. Fry rabbit in oil until golden brown. When brown on all sides, pour off excess oil. Add diced onion and lemon juice. Place lid on skillet and reduce heat. Slow cook until meat is tender. Check meat from time to time to make sure it isn't sticking to the bottom of the pan. Add a small amount of water if you want to steam the meat. Enjoy!

Many years ago people were told not to eat a rabbit in any month that did not contain an "R" in its name. Example: May, June, July or August. The reasoning is because people at that time ate wild rabbits. During the warmer months rabbits were susceptible to rabbit fever. This disease can be transmitted to humans. All months that contain an "R" are the colder months. Example: January, February, March, April, September, October, November and December. During these months the sickly rabbits would die off and only the healthy rabbits survived, lessening the chance of catching this disease.

SAC and FOX

(Asakiwaki) (Meskwaki)
Meaning: Yellow earth people   *Meaning: Red earth people*

The Sac and Fox people were two separate tribes that merged into a single tribe. They both spoke the same language and were indigenous to the same eastern woodlands and prairie regions of Michigan and Wisconsin. Today, most Sac and Fox people live in Oklahoma, Kansas and Iowa. A famous Sac and Fox tribal member was Jim Thorpe, an Olympic gold medal winner. The Sac and Fox tribal headquarters are located in Stroud, Oklahoma

Marinated Porcupine Chops

6 porcupine chops   1 quart maple sap (syrup)
1 small wild onion diced   4 wild leeks
salt to taste

In a non-metallic bowl, add maple sap (syrup) and diced onion. To this mixture, place porcupine chops one at a time with a wild leek between each chop. Marinate overnight in a cool place. In the morning, grease a stone griddle (skillet) with fat (cooking oil). When hot, remove the chops from marinate and fry. Serve hot on corn cakes.

Corn Cakes

2 handfuls cornmeal   2 fingers salt
¼ cup boiling water

Mix cornmeal and salt in a small bowl. Add boiling water to make a stiff dough. With cornmeal on your hands roll the dough into balls. Flatten the balls between your palms to make a round flat cake. Dip fingers in cold water and rub the cake to give it a very smooth surface. Place on a greased griddle and cook for about 10 minutes on each side or until dough is done in the middle. Serve hot.

SEMINOLE

(She-minn-ole)
Meaning: Wild

Seminole people are indigenous to Florida. Seminole and Muscogee Creek tribes are closely related. During the 1800's many Seminoles were removed from Florida to Indian Territory. Seminole people are noted for their colorful patchwork designs on their clothes. Oklahoma and Florida Seminole Nations have separate headquarters. Oklahoma Seminole tribal headquarters are located in Wewoka, Oklahoma. Florida Seminole tribal headquarters are located in Hollywood, Florida.

Seminole Hominy Corn

1 quart wood ashes or 4 heaping tablespoons powdered lime
4 quarts water
2 quarts dry corn kernels

Use granite or enamel pot. Never make hominy in an iron pot. Stainless steel is okay since it is not reactive to the lime or ash.

If using wood ashes: Boil ashes and water for 30 minutes. Keep stirring until the mixture stops bubbling. Strain through a cheesecloth or flour sack.

If using lime: Dissolve the powdered lime in the water and bring to a boil. No need to strain it.

To either method, add 2 quarts of corn kernels or as much corn as the water will cover. Cook until the hulls loosen from the kernels. Stir occasionally to keep corn from sticking to the bottom of the pan. Remove corn from stove and drain the liquid off. Wash the corn with fresh water until all the hulls can be floated off the top and the ash or lime taste is gone. Enjoy!

SHAWNEE

(Shaawanwaki Sia Wano Ki/Shaawanwaki Lenaweek)
Meaning: Southerner

Historically the Shawnee people inhabited Kentucky, Ohio, Indiana, Virginia, West Virginia, western Maryland and Pennsylvania. They are believed to be descendants of the mound builders. The most famous mound is the "Serpent Mound" located in Ohio. Today there are three federally recognized Shawnee tribes. Their headquarters are located in Oklahoma.

Shawnee Pudding

2 cups milk
1/3 cup molasses
1/3 cup cornmeal
1 egg slightly beaten
¼ cup granulated sugar

2 tablespoons butter
½ tablespoon ground ginger
½ teaspoon cinnamon
¼ teaspoon salt

In a sauce pan, on medium heat, combine milk and molasses. Stir in cornmeal. Cook and stir until bubbly. Reduce heat to low. In a separate bowl combine egg, sugar, butter, ginger, cinnamon and salt. Gradually stir this mixture into milk, molasses and cornmeal. Pour mixed ingredients into a buttered casserole dish. Bake at 300 degrees F. for 30 minutes.

SHOSHONE

(Newe)
Meaning: People

The Shoshone people are indigenous to Idaho, Nevada, Wyoming, Montana, Utah and parts of California. There are nine different Shoshone tribes today. The California Shoshone people had a plant based diet consisting of pine nuts, roots and seeds. They also hunted antelopes and rabbits. Headquarters for the Timbisha Shoshone tribe of California is located in Bishop, California.

Pine Nut Cakes

1 cup pine nuts
1/3 cup powdered milk
1 cup whole wheat flour
½ cup water
lard or cooking oil to cover bottom of skillet
½ teaspoon salt

Grind nuts until they are very finely ground. This can be done in a food processor. Add powdered milk, wheat flour and salt to the pine nuts. Mix ingredients thoroughly. Slowly pour water into mixture and continue to stir. If using a food processor, pulse 5-6 times and scrape down the sides of the container. Continue mixing until you can form a dough ball. Pinch off large walnut size pieces and roll into balls. Press, one at a time, in the palm of your hand. Shape into a small pancakes ¼ to ½ inch thick. Cover bottom of skillet with ½ inch oil. Drop cakes into hot oil. Don't crowd cakes. Brown the dough patties on each side. Drain on wire rack or paper towel. These cakes are best when eaten hot.

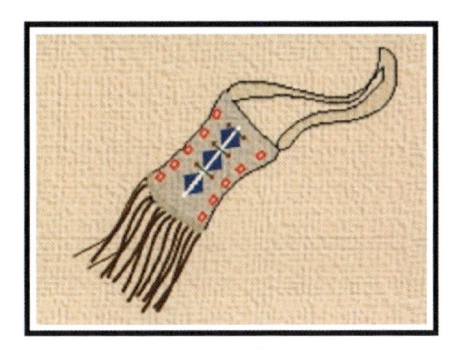

SIOUX

(Su)
Meaning: Little snakes

The original Lakota/Dakota homelands were located in an area of the United States now known as Wisconsin, Minnesota and North and South Dakota. Today, most Sioux people live in the Dakotas, Minnesota and Nebraska. Departments for Sioux tribal relations are located at Pine Ridge, South Dakota.

Wagmiza Wasna
(cornmeal pemmican)

2 cups yellow cornmeal	1 cup raisins
1 cup shortening or lard	1/3 cup sugar

Toast cornmeal until golden brown in a skillet stirring to prevent burning. Heat oil in a sauce pan. Grind raisins and mix with heated oil. Mix all ingredients together with sugar. Form into bite size pieces.

This cornmeal pemmican can be eaten by the handful like candy. It is chewy on the inside and crisp on the outside.

WICHITA

(wih-chih-taw)
Meaning: Name of a tribal town

The Wichita people are indigenous to an area of the United States now known as southern Oklahoma and northern Texas. The Wichita people built tall beehive-shaped houses thatched with grass. After the Europeans arrived, population pressures forced them further north into Kansas. Today, most Wichita people live in Oklahoma. The Wichita tribe does not have a permanent headquarters but can be contacted through the Mid-America All-Indian Center, 650 North Seneca Street, Wichita, Kansas

Wichita Honey Bee Icing

1 cup sugar
1 egg white, stiffly beaten
½ cup honey
1/8 teaspoon salt
¾ cup chopped marshmallows
½ teaspoon vanilla
1/3 cup water

Combine honey, sugar, water and salt. Place on stove and boil until it reaches the soft ball stage. (238 degrees F.) Add marshmallows. Beat and pour into beaten egg white very slowly. Add vanilla and beat until thick and creamy. This icing is very good on most cakes.

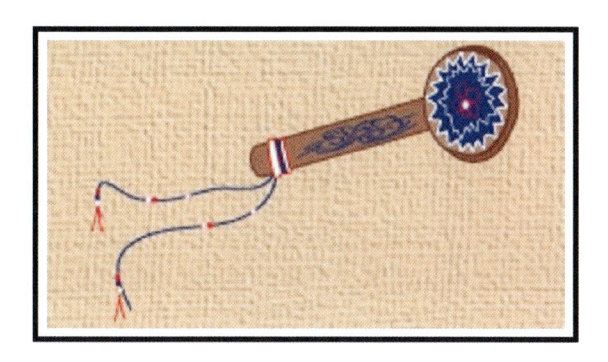

YAQUI

(Yoeme)
Meaning: Unhesitating people

The Yaqui people are indigenous to the valley of the Rio Yaqui in northern Mexico. Many Yaqui still live in their ancestral homeland. The Pascua Yaqui tribe is based in Tucson, Arizona.

Tamales

1 package of dried corn husks
chicken or pork
broth from meat (approximately 3 quarts)
1 pint lard
cayenne pepper
chili powder
masa harina (finely ground corn found near the flour on the grocery store shelf.)
salt to taste

Soak corn husks in warm water to soften. Cook chicken or pork in pot of water until tender and falls off the bone. When meat is done, pour off broth and set aside. Bone meat and shred into small pieces and place in a skillet with enough broth to cover the meat. Cook and season meat with cayenne pepper, chili powder and salt to taste. Cook until most of the broth is absorbed into meat. Add lard to remaining broth and stir until it is melted. If you don't have enough liquid, you can use canned chicken broth. Add cayenne pepper, salt, and chili to broth and stir. Keep adding masa harina until the mixture is the consistency of thick gravy. Drain water off corn husks and using one husk at a time, spread a small amount of masa over the husk. You can make this as thick or thin as you like. When masa is spread on husks, place an ample amount of meat in the center of the masa. Fold husks so that the meat is in the center of the tamale. Place tamale in a steamer and cook until done. About 30 minutes.

ZUNI

Ashiwi
Meaning: The flesh people

The Zuni people are natives of New Mexico. Unlike many other Native American tribes, the Zuni were never forced to leave their homelands and they are still living there today. The Zuni traded regularly with other tribes of the southwest. The Zuni trade routes reached into Mexico and to the California coast. Zuni artists are famous for their beautiful pottery and animal shaped fetish carvings. Zuni headquarters are located at Zuni, New Mexico.

Zuni Jackrabbit Stew

1 fat young jackrabbit (I would use a nice farm fed tender rabbit)
¼ cup cooking oil
2 cups hominy corn
2 sweet peppers, cut in half and seeded
6 carrots (diced)
1 large onion, chopped
½ tablespoon chili powder
1 ½ cups flour
4 teaspoon salt

Cut rabbit into serving size pieces. Salt each piece and coat with flour. Pour oil into a large cast iron pot and heat until the oil is smoking slightly. Brown rabbit pieces on each side in oil. Drain off extra oil. Add a little water to the pan and simmer for two hours. Then put hominy, peppers, carrots, onion and chili powder into pot and simmer until the carrots are done.

WillowVistaBooks.com

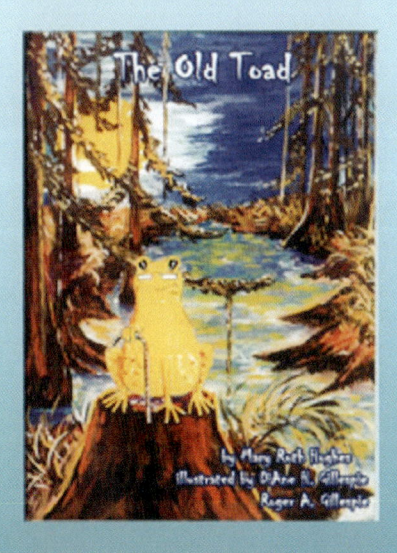

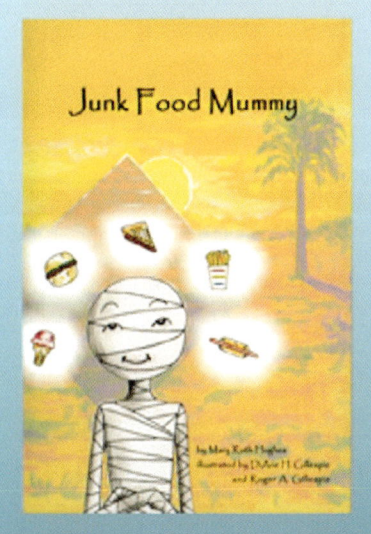

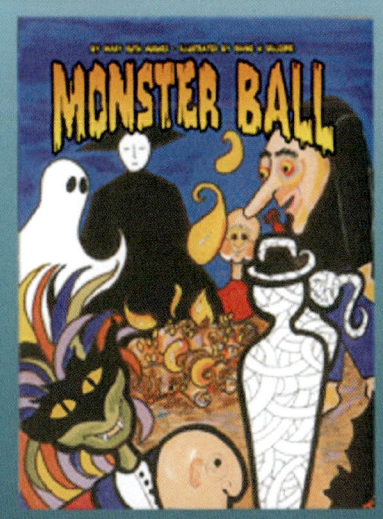

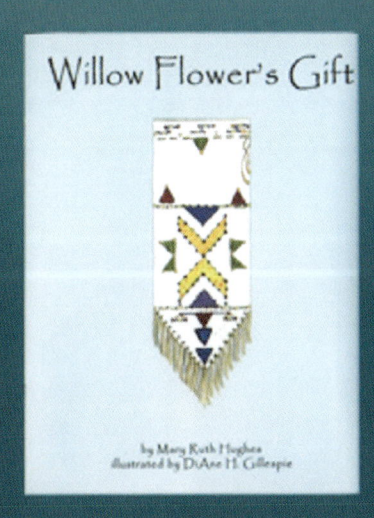

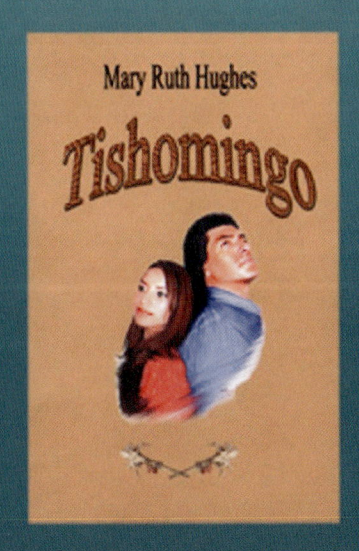

Printed in Poland
by Amazon Fulfillment
Poland Sp. z o.o., Wrocław